TIZA JOSEPH NYIRENDA

ZAMBIA'S STORY OF UNBRIDLED CAPITALISM AND LOST REVENUES

Copyright © 2017 by Tiza Joseph Nyirenda

Published in 2019 by Tiza Joseph Nyirenda

Book cover design and typesetting by Gregg Davies (www.greggdavies.com)

ISBN 9781727022889

The moral right of the author has been asserted. No part of this publication may be reproduced, distributed, or transmitted in any form or by any means, including photocopying, recording, or other electronic or mechanical methods, without the prior written permission of the author, except in the case of brief quotations embodied in critical reviews and certain other non-commercial uses permitted by copyright law.

"There are three things in this world which deserve no mercy, hypocrisy, fraud, and tyranny."
Frederick William Robertson, also known as Robertson of Brighton, an Anglican cleric.

Acknowledgments

My sincere gratitude to all who supported my writing from the very beginning to its publication, to my young sister, Taonga, My friend Pastor Roberts Liardon from Orlando Florida USA ,Dr.pZimba from Kitwe, MrsMbuzi of Macha health Institute of Sciences and Mr.Chileshe from Kitwe, am really humbled and thankful for your support.

Preface

When I was in third year at the Zambia Catholic University, pursuing my Bachelor's of Arts in Economics , the university organized a trip to Little Kitwe Theater, in Kitwe Town, to watch the documentary; Stealing Africa, Why poverty? (2013). It is a documentary that shows how Zambia has failed to capitalize on its natural resources, It shows how poverty, extreme environmental damage and under-investments in local agency and oversight sustain very high financial outflows from copper mining in Zambia. The documentary narrates how western individuals and their communities profit obscenely from personal and institutional dealings in Zambia. Christopher Guldbrandsen documentary, mentions further that USD29 Billion is being expatriated from Zambia to Switzerland, every year. To me the documentary was an eye opener about the unprecedented wave of plunder and pillage of resources going on in my country. It was so sad to watch and learn that Zambia,despite having abundant copper reserves, those who mainly benefitted from the copper revenues where the shareholders of the Multi-Nationals companies who run the copper mines in Zambia. "This is unacceptable," I said to myself. We of this Generation need to reverse the status quo, we need to make sure that Zambians benefit from their natural resources instead of the shareholders of the multinational companies.

As I watched the documentary one thing was made clear to me; Zambia is blessed with abundant natural resources that can bring significant social and economic development. One reason why the mineral wealth of Zambia has not significantly contributed to the long-term economic and social development agenda, is that Multi-National corporations who run the mines are engaged in tax avoidance schemes like transfer pricing and mis-invoicing. Tax avoidance of this nature is robbing the country significant amounts of money that can have an enormous positive impact on the social and economic development of Mother Zambia.After this trip I began to research further to see what has been going on in our country, as far as, the management of natural resources is concerned. That researched birthed this book. One thing is should be made clear, we shall continue to wallow in poverty, until, we as a country, can offer our own economic growth road map that will need a dedicated and honest political management team. We need to draft policies and legislations for utilizing our natural resources sustainably and sharing them more equitably.

Contents

Introduction   xiii

1. Poor Design of Development Agreements   1
2. Transfer Pricing Schemes by Multi-National Corporations   11
3. Government and Stakeholders Efforts to Clamp Down Transfer Pricing   29
4. Copper Revenues can be Drivers for Industrial Diversification   35
5. Zambia can become a Successful Welfare State if we can Experience Good Governance   49
6. Leadership is Key   61
7. Conclusion   73

BIBLIOGRAPHICAL REFERENCES AND NOTES   79

Introduction

International NGOs have raised concern that Zambia could be losing US$3billion every year in avoided corporate tax revenues. War-on-want, an organization that fights against the root causes of poverty and human rights violation globally released a Zambia tax report which revealed that in 2012 the amount of tax avoided by Mining companies every year amounts to US$2 billion, which represents 10% of Zambia's GDP. The mining sector is the chief culprit in avoiding tax obligations. Another organization based in the United States of America (America/USA) called Global Finance Integrity, which has pioneered recent research into illicit financial flows, estimates that US$8.8 billion left Zambia from the proceeds of crime; corruption and tax evasion in the 10 years between 2001- 2010-An average of US$880 million a year.

These illicit outflows are in addition to the US$2billion outflows from corporate tax avoidance noted by the Government with the help of International organizations like War-on-Want and Global finance Integrity. This brings us to the conclusion that approximately US$3billion a year is being lost. This is as a result of unbridled capitalism(lack of capacity on the part of the Government and very few legislation to curtail tax avoidance and) which came with the advent of liberalization.

In the 1990s the mines were privatized but the contracts signed with the new owners of the Mines were extremely generous to the effect that the mines did not contribute any reasonable revenues to the government in terms of corporate taxes. Zambian Privatization has been hailed by international organizations;Zambia in the books of the Bretton woods institutions isreported to have sold many state owned companies, especially in the mining sector, in a very short period of time, than any other country.

Rather than being a blessing to this country privatization became a nightmare, people lost jobs and the mines contribution to the state coffer in the next ten years or more was virtually absent. Some companies that were bought by foreign investors later became white elephants after the investors pulled out. Zambian privatization was hurriedly done, because they are some other countries who began the process of Privatization many years ago but still today, the process is still ongoing . Some political leaders in those countries are even thinking of getting back some of the companies they privatized because the benefits from those companies in private hands no longer accrue to the people of the country. Consider Britain, where now the majority of the population supports renationalization of rail, water and Mail services because these services have deteriorated, the prices of these services have gone very high and only shareholders benefit. The documentary; Stealing Africa… why poverty?(Guldbrandsen 2013) www.youtube.com/watch?v=WNYemui-AOfU, shows poverty, extensive environmental damaged and very high financials outflow from the copper mines in Zambia, due to lack of capacity on the part of the Government to curtail tax dodging. This makes me conclude that Zambia's privatization program was a rip-off because some of the investors that came lacked integrity and took advantage of the situation. The Zambian Government is losing money in billions that should have an enormous impact in an economy where 60% of the people live below the poverty datum line. The methods most companies use to evade tax are so complex; therefore it has been hard for the Zambian government authorities to clamp down some of their dirty tricks.

In this book I give an account of how our country has lost revenues particularly from the mining sector. The monies should have invested in our economy to support development but instead was drained out. I also look at the experience of other countries like Chile who produce copper like Zambia and what we can learn from the policies they put forth so that fiscal rents from their mineral resources benefit the nationals. I suggest adopting some of these policies for the good of mother Zambia and for posterity. Therefore this book is called *'The Story of Zambia's Unbridled Capitalism and Lost Revenues'* because it narrates how Zambia lost out or failed to capitalize the God given mineral resources. This book is written to engage Zambians into thinking objectively about how they would want the national economy to be run.. It cannot be overemphasized, Zambians must decide to manage their natural resources responsibly and accountably and use them for the common good of every Zambian. Zambia needs a better deal on its natural resources so that the native Zambians who own the natural resources can benefit.; Of course that can only happen if Zambians can resolve to provide leadership that is responsible, accountable and incorruptible.

Make no mistake, Zambia has the wealth and resources to organize our economy so everyone can lead a decent life, with a home to call their home,a job that pays enough to live on and the opportunities to succeed. This book is a humble attempt to remind ourselves that we are blessed with abundant natural resources which are being exploited. It is sad to see that these resources are not contributing, as they should be, to the nation's economic and social development agenda because they are being exploited.Our land is rich in natural resources, yet the majority of the Zambian people are poor. It is a paradox we should not entertain anymore.

Tiza Joseph Nyirenda

1

Poor Design of Development Agreements

In 1991, Zambia had a new president by the name of Dr. Frederick Titus Jacob Chiluba, of the Movement for Multiparty Democracy (MMD) who defeated Dr. Kenneth David Kaunda, of the United National Independent Party (UNIP), in the polls. There was a sense of hope among many Zambians that better things would follow, due to the change of governance system from one party state to multiparty democracy. The losing Candidate, Dr. Kaunda, had been in power for 27 long years. He had his failures and successes in the way he managed the economy. Dr. Kaunda pursued socialist policies from 1970 which saw the nationalization of the copper mines in the Early 1970s since copper accounted for 70% of the exports. This was done so that the Zambian people exercised sovereignty over their mineral resources. This also helped secure a large proportion of Mineral revenues as compared to the situation before nationalization, when the mines were in private hands.

State ownership of the mining assets was used as a tool to increase the government receipts from mineral rents to foster development in other sectors of the Zambian economy. I believe this was a good move because the metal prices on the international market were high, but the timing was wrong.

Shortly after nationalizing the mines in 1975, the price of copper fell, which marked the beginning of the country's three decades long economic stagnation. The oil crisis of the early 1970s caused world commodity prices to collapse, as global demand dropped. Low demand for copper meant that Zambia's export earnings declined and rising oil prices meant that the country had to spend more on oil imports. So all hope of benefitting from mineral revenues from state owned copper mines was lost for three decades as a result of low copper prices and other factors.

The decline in mining sector fortunes cannot be attributed exclusively to the process of Nationalization as some tend to think. Just like I have said before, that nationalizing the mines would have helped Zambia maximize mineral revenues, but this happened at a time when the price of copper fell on the international market. It is also good to note that it was not only Zambia that was affected by the fall in copper prices, but all copper dependent countries like Chile felt the economic stress.

Between the periods 1970-1975,1976-1990 and 1991-1999, per capita GrossDomestic Product (GDP) fell by -0.8, -3.1 and -7.2% respectively. The average Zambian was becoming poorer and poorer as the years went by, given that the Zambian population was increasing at a faster rate than the GDP. This saw revenues from the copper industry decline as a result of the low copper price and mismanagement of the state owned copper mines.

To finance the social programs in the country, the Zambian government relied on Aid and external borrowing. The World Bank believed that the collapse of copper prices wastemporal and so encouraged Zambia to borrow to mitigate the negative effects on health and Education services,and food and industrial requirements. However as government spending began to increase and copper prices did not recover, Zambia's debt soared. By as early as 1984, Zambia was the most indebted country in the world relative to its GDP.

By the time Dr.Chiluba took office in 1991, the economy was in doldrums. Quick reforms were needed to revival the ailing economy. Copper prices had hit rock bottom and the debt to the World Bank and the International Monetary Fund (IMF) was so large that Zambia could not get new loans. For the Bretton Woods Institution to give Zambia more money and debt relief they made a series of policy conditions attached to new loans and debt relief. The government was running out of cash, so they had no choice but to adhere to conditions set by the foreign donors. This weakened the country's ability to set its own policies for the next twenty years.

One policy condition was Liberalization of the economy and privatization of the Mines because the state owned company ZCCM was making losses. Privatization of the state owned mining company was claimed to hold the key to turning the economy around in the medium term.

In 1997 the government started the process of privatizing the mines. In the case of Zambia's privatization all the mines were bought by foreign investors, not a single Zambian bought a mine because there were few Zambians companies with the wealth to buy a copper mine. This placed ownership of the mines in foreign hands and this makes it likely that profits from the copper mines leave the country without any positive impact on the Zambian economy to spend on rebuilding the nation.

However when the Zambian government began privatizing the mines, the foreign companies which wanted to buy the mines had an upper hand in the negotiation, simply because the Zambian side was represented by incompetent politicians to the effect that the State owned company(ZCCM) assets were undervalued, coupled with the fact that the mines had dilapidated infrastructure and declining copper prices on the international Market .

Through negotiations which were dubbed "Development Agreements," generous concessions were handed out to the new owners of Zambia's mining assets. The companies negotiated to pay lower corporate tax than that which applied to other industries. Corporate taxes were set at 25% compared to 35% paid by companies in other sectors of the economy. The royalty tax rate was capped at 3% on gross copper proceeds far less compared to what was obtaining in other copper producing countries. Loss carry-forward provision extended up to 15-20 years.

The most controversial close in the development agreements was the length of the 'stability period' of between 15 and 20 years during which the agreed terms and conditions were not to be varied.The mining investors where clever to put this in the agreements, because this clause was going to favor them.The privatization program ended in 2000.

During the same period the price of copper on the international market recovered beginning in 2003 and ending in mid-2008because of the financial crisis. However it is important to note that the Zambian government did not fiscally significantly benefit from the boom as a result of the recovery in copper prices due to the poor design of the Development Agreements among other things.

The mining company contributed to the government

through taxes paid by its employees in the form of Pay-As-You-Earn tax. When it came to corporate taxes, the mining companies contributed very little. This made Zambia lose the needed tax revenue from the mining sector to invest in other sectors of the economy. Chile which is the largest copper producing country fiscally benefitted from the boom of 2003 to 2008.Copper's share of fiscal revenues in Chile has been in the range of 20.7% to 31.1% peaking in 2006 at 31.1%.During the same period, in Zambia, revenues from copper, as a share of total fiscal revenue were equal to or below 1%. The poor design of the Development Agreements embodying generous tax and other concessions precluded Zambia from generating reasonable revenues from the copper boom. It was until 2008, when the mining fiscal regime was revisited, when the share rose to 3.4%.

What is most shocking about this period is that despite the increase in the production of copper in Zambia and the high copper prices, copper's share of fiscal revenues was far small compared to that enjoyed in the 1980s and 1990s when the copper prices were low and copper production in Zambia decreased. Between 1980 and 1990, the level of copper production in Zambia decreased at an annual rate of -3.4 to -5.0 per year.

However during the same period(1980-1990) copper production in Zambia contributed an average of 5.1% to total fiscal revenues. It was after 1994 when the revenues decreased to 2%. After 2000 copper production peaked and in 2003 copper prices rose sharply, but revenues from the mines which had been privatized was a joke. Between 2003 and 2007 copper production in Zambia contributed 1% or below the total fiscal revenues. It was after 2008 when the fiscal regime was revised, that the percentage of revenues from copper production rose to 3%. But that is still less than the contribution between 1980 and 1990 when the mines were in state hands and copper prices and production were low.

This is the irony of the situation; Zambian copper mines were contributing more when in government hands when output and prices were on the downward trend than when under private ownership when output and prices were on the upward trend.

Zambia when compared to other copper producing countries lost out on revenues from the mining sector. When other copper producing countries were benefitting from the boom in copper prices Zambia benefitted less. The story that has emerged is somehow ironic. Despite the positive production and price trends, the fiscal impact of the boom in the mining sector has been weak. Zambia's fiscal benefit from the boom in the prices of copper was virtually absent. The relationship between export dependence on natural resources and revenue generation is captured in the diagram below.

. . .

FISCAL REVENUE AND EXPORT EARNINGS IN RESOURCE-RICH LOW AND MIDDLE INCOME COUNTRIES (Average 2006-2010)

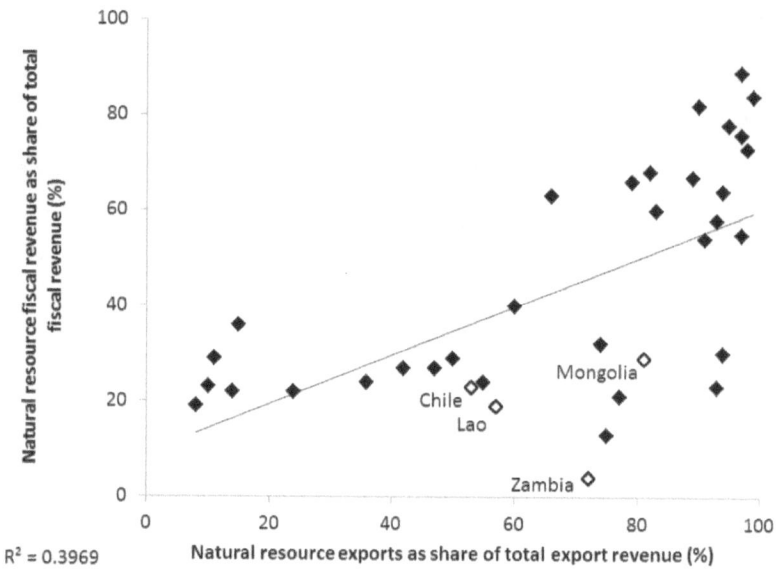

Source: Data is from IMF (2012b)

Zambia seems to diverge from the trend, with extreme low revenue generation relative to its export dependence, even when compared with other low-income copper producers.

For Example, according to the United States Geological Survey(USGS), Mineral resources program, basing 2012, as the year of estimate, Mongolia is ranked the 17th Copper producer in the world, producing 121,000 metric tonnes of Copper, while, Lao is ranked the 26th in terms of copper production, producing 60,000 metric tonnes of Copper. Zambia is ranked the 8th in copper production in the world, producing 515,000 tonnes of Copper in 2012, at the time the above graph was made. One might ask, "why is that Zambia diverge from the trend, with low extreme revenue collection relative to its export dependence, when compared to low-income Copper producers like Mongolia and Lao?" The poor design of the Development Agreements embodying generous tax and other concessions precluded the country from generating meaningful revenues from the Copper Boom period.

However some Zambians were angry at the whole situation, particularly those in the copper producing areas or towns. They vetted their anger in the general elections of 2006, when most people from the copper producing areas voted for opposition candidate Michael Chilufya Sata of the Patriotic Front (PF) party because he campaigned against the development agreements.

The MMD Government which was in power tried to renegotiate the development agreements, but they faced enormous challenges. This is because of the stability period which stipulated that the agreements could not be varied, amended, cancelled or terminated during the agreed period. The other problem was that the agreements were agreed on a bilateral basis.

It would be in 2008 when the periods specified in the development agreements would expire and the government would renegotiate these contracts individually by passing new registration called; "the Mines and Mineral act of 2008" which saw contribution of revenues from the mines rise to 3% of the total fiscal revenues. But the story of how Zambia lost out does not end with the development agreements. It also extends to the transfer pricing scheme which has made Zambia to continue to lose billions of dollars every year.

2

Transfer Pricing Schemes by Multi-National Corporations

Transfer pricing or transfer mispricing by multinationals corporations is an evil in our society that has made it possible for Zambians to further lose billions of dollars every year. The booming copper prices between 2003 and 2008 should have made Zambia benefit substantially from corporate taxes paid by these multi-national groups who run the mines but this did not happen largely due to transfer pricing schemes.

Transfer pricing or transfer mispricing is done by shifting your profits out of a high tax country like Zambia where the profits are made and shift them artificially to tax havens countries where they will not be taxed very much. The way this is done by multi-national groups is that, they have subsidiaries all over the world and these subsidiaries trade with each other. And they can manipulate the prices of these trades for booking keeping or accounting purposes. The tax haven subsidiary will buy something cheaply from a subsidiary which is in a country with high taxations and sell it at a higher price on the International market were prices are determined by demand and supply and between that gap there is a huge profit which will not be taxed in the tax haven.

On paper this makes Switzerland the biggest importer of Zambian copper, but that does not mean the copper is physically shipped from Zambia to Switzerland, the documentation goes to Switzerland but the copper goes all over the world.

It does not surprise me that Glencore(a Swiss-based company) was implicated in the Transfer pricing scandal.

Glencore is one of the world's largest extractive companies and a producer and marketer of over 90 commodities worldwide. In Zambia Glencore manages Mopani copper mines, which consists of four underground copper and cobalt mines, a concentrator and a cobalt plant on the town of Kitwe and an underground mine, concentrator, smelter and refinery in the town of Mufulira, on the Copper-belt province of Zambia. Mopani is 90% owned by a company registered in the British Virgin Islands, which in turn is majority owned by Glencore Finance, registered in Bermuda.

In 2011, a report written by the Norwegian tax auditors-Grant Thornton and consulting firm Econ Poyri was leaked. Previously in 2009 the Zambia Revenue Authority (ZRA) had contracted the Two Norwegian Tax auditors, to investigate tax avoidance and tax evasion related to Mopani Copper Mine .

The Grant Thornton pilot audit report is available at

(Grant Thornton, *Pilot Audit Report – Mopani Copper Mines Plc*, 2011, available at

http://www.actionaid.org.uk/taxjustice/glencore-tax-dodging-in-zambia click on the link)

The report alleged that there had been an inexplicable increase in Mopani's declared costs between 2006 and 2008 and inconsistencies in the production volumes declared. In the five years 2007-11, for example, Mopani's annual reports suggest that it produced $4.3 billion worth of copper. Using the U.S Geological survey however, this production would have been worth US$6.8 billion. This means that Mopani's own sales figures are reduced in order to reduce their taxable income.

Further the audit report by Grant Thornton alleged that Glencore was engaging in transfer pricing activities and that its sales of copper to related parties were not in accordance with the Organization of Economic Development and Cooperation (OECD).

The OECD guidelines under its Arm's length principle stipulates that " Transactions should be valued as if they had been carried out between unrelated parties, each acting in his own best interest" (OECD, 2006), and this clause was embedded in the 'Development agreements'.

Transfer pricing is not problematic,as long as the price that is set between subsidiaries, matches the "arm's length" price at which a transaction would have taken place between unrelated parties. However transfer pricing may become abusive or illegal when related parties seek to distort the prices as a means of reducing their overall tax bill.

The audit alleged that Mopani sold copper at below market - prices(At quarter of the official prices quoted at the London metal exchange) to Glencore in Switzerland. Then the Swiss based company sells the copper at world prices as if it originated from Switzerland, (netting the price difference as profit while consistently reporting losses in Zambia). This means Glencore shifted its profits from Zambia to Switzerland were they will were taxed at a very low rate because of Switzerland's low tax regime.

Further the audit concluded that the Mopani cost structure cannot be trusted to represent the true nature of the costs of the Mopani mining operation and that Mopani had resisted the pilot audit at every stage. The auditors found that the company overestimated operating costs, compared to other firms in the industry. Glencore responded to the allegations in the audit report saying

" We refute the conclusions of this draft report and we question the reasons for the manner in which it was leaked".

See Jamie Doward, 'Glencore denies allegations over copper mine tax', The Observer, 17 April 2011

http://www.theguardian.com/business/2011/apr/17/glencore-deniescopper-tax-allegations?INTCMP=ILCNETTXT3487.

See also Glencore evidence to the UK Parliament's

International Development Committee, April 2012,

http://www.publications.parliament.uk/pa/cm201213/cmselect/cmintdev/130/130we18.htm

This is in line with what David Manley former economist at the Zambia revenue Authority is reported to have noted, that no one, except the mining companies themselves, knows what the costs of production really are.

This is because there are no governmental officials permanently stationed at mine sites, or check points to verify production, export volumes and mineral grade. According to government officials, they are on record agreeing that the government does not know how much it costs to extract a ton of copper for any company, what the grade is, or what the value is of the additional metals coming out of the process. Instead it has to rely on company reports which may be falsified.

Research undertaken in 2013 showed that in previous years, up to half of Zambia copper exports had been destined for Switzerland, according to Zambia customs, but according to Swiss import data, none of it ever arrived.

Switzerland merely serves as the site for buying and selling of copper contracts without any physical trade in copper ore or copper in any stage of processing. In addition, exports of copper from Switzerland have much higher declared prices than those in Zambia. This means Switzerland exports copper from Zambia to the London metal exchange at a higher price than it was exported from Zambia to Switzerland.

War on want, Zambia tax report, shows that if Zambia had secured the same price for its copper exports as Switzerland in 2008, for example, the value would have been nearly six times higher adding US$11.4 billion to Zambia's GDP. It is for this reason that Glencore has become the most criticized company in the world for tax avoidance, among other issues.

This means that the people benefitting from the Zambia's copper are not Zambians and I strongly believe this does not please God the almighty, who gave us this natural resource called copper. It is for this reason that Pope Francis called unbridled capitalism the dung of the devil. Lost revenues means lost opportunities to improve the living standards of the Zambian people through adequately funding all key sectors of Government. Zambia has the second largest copper reserves in Africa yet even in times when the price of copper booms, evidently, the benefits of the boom do not accrue to the Zambian people but to a few individual who have gotten wealthy as a result of looting Zambia copper.

If Zambia had benefit extensively from our copper deposits between the years 2003 -08,and if the money could have been used prudently, this nation would have seen massive reductions in poverty levels, . The percentage living below the poverty datum line would not have been 60% of the entire population.

Like mentioned earlier in the introduction to this book; War- on- want, an organization that fights against the root causes of poverty and human rights violation globally released a Zambia tax report that revealed that in 2012 the amount avoided by companies every year amounts to US$2 billion, which represents 10% of Zambian GDP.

IN NOVEMBER 2012, Zambia,s then deputy Finance Minister, Mr. Miles Sampa also confirmed the findings by war-on-want when he made the extra-ordinary announcement that Zambia was losing $2billion a year in tax avoidance.

The mining sector cited to be the chief culprit in avoidance of tax obligations. He went on to shade more light on the statement by making it clear that of all the copper mining houses in Zambia, only one or two were declaring positive earnings and the other mining houses for one reason or another, some genuine, some not, are always making losses.

Check the link below

Matthew Hill, 'Zambia Says Tax Avoidance Led by Miners Costs $2 Billion a Year', 25 November 2012,

http://www.bloomberg.com/news/2012-11-25/zambia-says-taxavoidance-led-by-miners-costs-2-billion-a-year.html

A US based organization, Washington based think tank- Global Finance Integrity, which has pioneered recent research into illicit financial flows, estimates that US$8.8 billion left Zambia from the proceeds of crime, corruption and tax evasion in the 10 years between 2001-2010- An average of $880 million a year.

Check the link below.

Sarah Freitas, Global Financial Integrity, 13 December 2012,

http://www.financialtransparency.org/2012/12/13/what-billions-in-illicit-and-licit-capital-flight-means-for-thepeople-of-zambia/

These illicit outflows are in addition to the $2billion

outflows from corporate tax avoidance noted by the government. This brings us to the conclusion that approximately US$3billion a year has been lost. The loss of approximately $3billion a year is equivalent to nearly half of Zambia's entire annual Government budget of ZMW32.2 billion (US$5.9 billion) in 2013 alone.

It is also equivalent to nearly twice of Zambia's combined spending on health and Education of ZMW9.26 billion or US$1.69 billion. This means our health sector; education sector and other sector's budgets would have doubled. This would have financed activities to help achieve the Millennium Development Goals. Money would have been available to finance the country infrastructure deficit which was estimated to be at US$500 million in 2013, which means that the amount of taxes forgone were four times than the Infrastructure deficit. There was going to be no need of going to the capital markets to issue bonds like we did a few years ago.

To meet this financing gap in infrastructure development the government issued a euro bond in September 2012 and raised US$750 million. The bond issuance pushed the government's external debt stock higher to US$3.2 billion in 2012 from US$2.0 billion representing an increase of 61 percent. Today, we struggling to repay the euro bonds.

In all this we must remember that when our forefathers fought for freedom, they envisioned a prosperous Zambia, were its citizens will use their natural resources they are endowed with, to uplift the standard of living in our country. The fight for self-rule was to restore the dignity that the British colonial masters had not respected. But today our dignity has been stripped by these multinationals that get copper from our country without paying a fair share of their tax obligations. This should be an insult to us as Zambians.

Vedanta

Another company which has been alleged to be dodging tax by way of transfer pricing is Vedanta, a registered company in London until this year 2018, with a head office in Mumbai India.

It manages three copper mines in Zambia, notably Konkola copper mines (KCM), Zambia largest and one of the largest high-grade copper ore bodies in the world. Vedanta corporate structure includes numerous subsidiaries in secret Jurisdictions; Its annual report for 2014 lists 29 subsidiaries in the tax havens countries such as Mauritius, the Netherlands, British Virgin Islands and Jersey.

On 4th July 2014,Mwalu, Kalaluka wrote a story in the defunct Post newspaper titled "KCM cheats on copper exports". The paper reported that Vedanta Resources-owned-Konkola copper mines(KCM) was cheating on its copper export prices by underpricing and selling it through subsidiaries in Dubai. The paper alleged that Vedanta used a Dubai-based subsidiary, Fujairah gold to buy undervalued copper from Konkola and thus hide its profits.

The article referred to an arbitration hearing in the London High Court of Justice that heard how Vedanta had allegedly used a Dubai based subsidiary, Fujaira Gold, to buy under-valued copper from Konkola and thus hid its profits. But a Konkola spokesperson denied the allegation.

It is probably for this reason that while Vedanta paid only ZK54000($11.111m) in corporation tax in 2011,but its annual reports states that its Zambia operations(which include two mines in addition to Konkola) generated $1.7-billion in revenues and an operating profit of $221million in 2011/12.

They were protestors who assembled at the Zambia High commission premises in London, demanding that Vedanta publicize its profits and taxes.

See http://www.foilvedanta.org/uncategorized/protests-atzambia-high-commission-demand-kcm-publish-profits-and-taxes/

Further in May 2014, a video posted on the internet caused further controversy for Vedanta, apparently showing Anil Agarwal, Vedanta's chief executive officer, mocking the Zambian government for selling Konkola

Copper Mine(KCM) for the knock-down price of US$25 million: the mines asking price at the time was US$400 million.

The video was taken at the Jain International Trade Organization meeting in Bengalum, India. Agarwal could be seen saying that the mine brings in a profit of US$500 million a year, a figure that does not exactly square with Vedanta's annual report stating that the company made a loss of US$6.3 million in the year ending march 2013.

Many Zambians were outraged and slammed Argawal,

See 'Zambia: Zambians slam Indian mining investor for mocking government', 18 May 2014,

http://www.africanmanager.com/site_eng/detail_article.php?art_id=21978

Here was Anil Agarwal caught on camera declaring that the company makes a profit when in Zambia, it was declaring losses. The story was on all media outlets in the country and I expected the government to prosecute Agarwal, use him as witness in Vedanta's tax fraud.

Investigations were launched of which the outcome most people do not know. I have never heard of a scenario where a thief confessed to you, that he/she stole your most valuable items and yet you let him go without full restitution, where on Earth?

We as a Christian nation should protect our natural

resources from being exploited and use the resources wisely, for the good of Mother Zambia; this is a divine assignment from God. These resources must generate income that will be shared equally among the Zambian people. As Christians we should understand that the nation of Israel went into exile several times not just because of personal sins of the children of Israel, but because of social sins like failing to seek justice, defend the oppressed, take up the cause of the fatherless, and plead the case of the widow (Isaiah 1:17).

Therefore failure by our leaders to seek justice for the Zambians does please God. Some Zambians think that by being quiet over the injustice that is happening is what it means to be a Christian nation.

On the contrary, being a Christian does not mean being passive and afraid, for the scriptures tells us that God has not given us a spirit of timidity but of power (2 Timothy 1:7). Passivity is of the devil not of God.

We should remember the words of an Anglican cleric, Frederick William Robertson also known as Robertson of Brighton; who said "There are three things in this world which deserve no mercy- hypocrisy, fraud, and tyranny".

A fellow Christian is telling us that fraud is among the things that deserve no mercy in the world, because it has the potential to destroy the destiny of a nation and its citizens. But here in Zambia, as a Christian nation we tolerate fraud that is robbing a decent standard of living to millions of Zambians who live in abject poverty.

The pillage and plunder of natural resources that is ongoing in the mining sector will mean that our children to be born will inherit a country whose natural resources would have been exploited. They will definitely ask questions like"where were our parents and grandparents when the wanton looting of natural resources was on going"?. They will be told that the past generation was a generation where people were passive. They knew who was stealing from their country but kept quiet. It will be an embarrassing moment, unless we do something now, there will be nothing left for posterity.

We must not think that we are a poor nation, on the contrary we are wealth, because we have the resources that other African countries do not have. For a start we have 15million people to tap from as a workforce. Then we have our soil and all that is underneath. Some countries with far less resources than we have are doing incredibly well. It is simply a matter of how we think and the leaders we have opted for.

However this should not be taken to mean all mining houses have not paid their fair share of taxes to the Government. In 2011 Government revenues from the mining sector rose significantly. This was due to tax changes brought in by the government that increased corporation tax and the royalty rate.

The Zambia Government earned US$1.35 billion in revenues from mining based on copper production worth US$7.23 billion. Half of all Government revenues came from one company Kansanshi Mining Plc., jointly owned by First Quantum (80%) and the Zambian Government (20%). It was during this period that our country Zambia was classified as a lower middle income country together with Ghana as a result of Zambia's upward adjustment in Zambia's income growth.

However during the same time that Kansanshi paid a fair share of their tax obligations, Glencore and African Barrick Gold paid no corporate tax at all, another mine owned by Vedanta only paid a token amount. Out of the five mining houses in Zambia, four of them, excluding Kansanshi, produced copper worth US$4.28 billion but paid a total of only US$310 million.

Zambia Sugar Plc.'s Tax Avoidance Schemes

It is not only the mining companies in Zambia that have been accused of tax avoidance. British company, Associated British Foods (ABF), owner of silver spoon sugar, Ryvita and Primark, has also been the subject of research alleging tax avoidance in Zambia.

In 2013 a detailed report, the result of a 12 month investigation by Action Aid, revealed that ABF subsidiary, Zambia sugar, had generated profits of $123 million but paid virtually nothing to the Zambian government.

Rather it had found legal ways to siphon $83.7million ($13million a year) a third of pre-tax tax profits out of Zambia into tax havens including Ireland, Mauritius and the Netherlands.

See 'ActionAid exposes tax avoidance by Associated British Food Group in Zambia', 14 February 2013,

http://www.actionaid.org.uk/news-and-views/actionaidexposes-tax-avoidance-by-associated-british-foodgroup-in-zambia

The research further went to reveal that ABF group was using a variety of tax avoidance techniques; ABF, after it had bought Zambia Sugar Plc. in 2007, paid its Irish arm over $47.6 million for 'management fees' despite the company financial statements stated that it had no employees. The company says this was an error; but in any case Zambia lost an estimated $7.4 million in corporate tax and withholding of taxes.

The report estimates that Zambia public services lost around $27million as a result of the corporate tax avoidance schemes and special tax breaks, enough money to put 48,000 children in school. The revenue to tax havens is 10 times larger than the amount the UK gives Zambia in Aid for education each year. However ABF denied the allegations.

See (ABF, 'Media statement on ActionAid report', 10 February 2013, http://www.abf.co.uk/media/news/ 2013/media_statement_on_actionaid_report

For ActionAid and ABF material on the case, see also

http://businesshumanrights.org/en/documents/ actionaid-report-into-tax-avoidance-byassociated-british-foods-in-zambia

3

Government and Stakeholders Efforts to Clamp Down Transfer Pricing

But this is not to say the Zambian government has not been doing anything to monitor the operations of these multi-nationals in a bid to end tax avoidance. In 2012 and 2013 government enacted two statutory instruments namely SI 33 and SI 55 to monitor international transactions.

SI 55 empowered the bank of Zambia to monitor inflows, outflows and international transactions. The SI 55 was meant to increase money supply and most likely lead to lowering interest rates, if government borrowing from banks was controlled. As a result of reduced interest rates, investment and production in the country was going to increase. This is because the legislation was meant to capture minerals from exports but also help in understanding how funds generated from exporting activities are externalized.

Among other requirements, exporters were supposed to deposit cash receipts into a foreign currency account held in a local commercial bank while foreign investors were required to deposit the cash of their pledged investment component in a similar account.

Further mining companies were required to declare the quantity and grade of minerals being exported. This was meant to help to arrive at an accurate value of mineral exports. However after few months of these instruments at work, government revoked the two statutory instruments due to the fall in the value of the national currency- the Kwacha. The minister of finance then, Mr. Alexander Chikwanda, blamed the fall of the Kwacha on a cartel hoarding dollars. I believe these are the same multinational corporations because foreign Investors are one of the largest supplier of foreign currency in the country. The belief is that investors withheld export earnings as a way of protesting against SI55.

There is a popular belief in Zambia that the mining companies are holding the country to ransom and I also believe it to be true. It is worth mentioning that with much of the industries privatized, even domestic financial markets depend on foreign investors. Therefore to some degree Exchange rate stability is contingent to the behavior of foreigners.

Zambia has also received considerable transfer pricing

technical assistance from western countries like Norway and the IMF, who have come on board to help Zambia tax authorities get the necessary skills to meet the challenges of transfer pricing, although, many feel it might take time for the Zambian authorities to gain the capacity to deal with these companies evading tax. In 2011, for example a cooperation program between the IMF and the Zambia Revenue Authority was established.

The Zambia Revenue Authority has allocated transfer pricing specialists to the mining and non-mining audit teams. As a result, they have developed sector specific transfer pricing expertise as well as overcome potential internal coordination challenges. A representative from the OECD visits Zambia multiple times each year, to provide top-up transfer pricing training and support, however David Manley, a former Economist at Zambia Revenue Authority, is on record saying that it will take time before Zambia's lack of capacity stops being a constraint on its fiscal losses.

To improve access to information on where mining companies are selling the copper, ZRA amended rule i8 of value added tax(VAT).

This brought in some developments in accessing information towards the operations of the mines. Before ZRA approved the sale as zero rated, companies were supposed to provide copies of export documents for the goods bearing a certificate of shipment provided by the

ZRA, tax invoices for the goods, bearing a certificate of shipment provided by ZRA, tax invoices for the goods exported, and proof of receipt of payment for the goods. Companies argued that it was almost impossible to provide that kind of documentation because they sold to Multinationals trading houses. It is for this reason why there was a row between mining houses and government over more than US$600 in VAT refunds which were withheld by the Government.

Further to counter tax avoidance by some companies some Zambian and International NGOs in 2011 filed a complaint to the Organization for Economic Cooperation and Development (OECD) Against Mopani Copper Mine Plc., claiming that Glencore's activities were violating the OECD guidelines for multinational enterprise.

The five NGOs were Centre for Trade policy and Development in Zambia, Sherpa in France, Berne Declaration in Switzerland, and Mining Watch Canada and L'Entraide Missionare, both in Canada. This is because the arm's length principle for economic cooperation and Development stipulates that "transactions should be valued as if they had been carried out between unrelated parties, each one acting on his own interest". (OECD, 2006). Yet the OECD ruling was inconclusive, simply concluding that the two set of parties agreed to disagree. However it has been observed that the risk of tax avoidance in the case of

Mopani is heightened by the fact that the mines ownership structure is mainly located in secrecy Jurisdictions.

But the other question would be that why didn,t these NGOs then bring the matter to legal institutions to settle the matter in Zambia? It has been observed by many that Zambia does not have a transfer pricing dispute resolution mechanism.

The ability of Multinational corporations to get away with tax dodging globally depends on the willingness of Governments around the world, especially those presiding over tax havens like the UK, which allows them to do what they are doing.

The western countries have created the mechanism by which this money flows into the western world countries coffers. Therefore western countries have the same responsibility to the poor country like Zambia, to stop tax avoidance and Transfer pricing. The Global financial integrity notes that the global shadow system; a network of secrecy laws, tax havens, shell corporations, and banks like HSBC without real money laundering controls, facilitates both illicit financial and pernicious corporate tax avoidance. We need to break the system down; we can start by reforming the international customs and trade protocols to detect and curtail trade miss-invoicing and to ensure that country by country submits reports of sales, profits and taxes paid by multinationals companies.

4

Copper Revenues can be Drivers for Industrial Diversification

We can not keep on crying over spilled milk-billions of dollars have already been lost. And if we do not take action today, more billions will be lost.

What we now need to do, is learn lessons from the story of how we have lost billions of dollars from the mining sector. We need policies and legislation so that what happened does not repeat itself. The Zambian Government need to play an active role in the metal industry. We need policies and legislation to stop what is reportedly happening.

One way the Government can play an active role in the metal industry is to increase their shareholding in any mining company. Currently the Government of Zambia through Zambia consolidated Copper mines Investment

Holdings(ZCCM-IH) have shares in the range of 20 to 30 in some of the mining companies, which is too small because with such a holding, the Government does not have any measure of control in the running of the mines. The Government should consider increasing their shareholding to 50% so that they can have an active role in the running of the mining houses. In that way they will be able to put measures or conditions that will protect our resources from being plundered by multinationals. Further they will be able to verify production costs and volume and copper grades. This will enhance transparency in the mining sector so that every investor in the mining sector pays a fair share of tax from what they are getting.

It cannot be overemphasized; Zambia should diversify its economy to accelerate economic development. Copper remains our country's main export constituting 70% of total exports since independence. However our dependency on copper has not translated into significant wealth creation and economic prosperity. The overreliance on a natural resource like copper to the detriment of creating other industries and diversifying the economy is called by development specialists and economists the "Resource Curse."

Without doubt the over-reliance on one commodity, copper, has negatively affected our country. We have failed to broaden our range of exports, developing open mechanisms and industries to add value to the commodities we produce, or support the entrepreneurial impulses. Therefore the growth of our economy has been stymied as a result of failing to diversify our economy. Because commodities such as copper depend on availability and as much as demand, they are subject to sometimes volatile price variations.

On the financing channel for the diversification framework, copper and other export revenues have not been addressed in the current framework. If the Zambian Government can play an active role in the mining industry, as I highlighted, it can realize fiscal rents from the mining industry, which can be used to promote industrial development in other sectors of the economy.Since we are talking of diversifying the economy to Agriculture and other non-metal sectors, we need significant amounts of money to make the diversification program successful. We need to mechanize the agriculture sector, increase agriculture inputs, fund research and development in Agriculture, develop the irrigation system so that farmers can grow crops all year round etc. All these require a substantial amount of money to actualize.

So the next question is, where are we going to source funds for these projects?. Mind you, the national debt levels have risen so high to the extent where further borrowing is not healthy for the economy. The funding for industrial diversification could partly come from copper and other minerals related revenues. . A High taxation policy could be one fiscal policy the Government of Zambia can use to mobilize financial resources that can be used to accelerate economic and social development of this country. However, a high taxation policy can hamper the expansion of the mining industry. High tax rates in a developing country like Zambia has limits; if you have higher taxation levels, particularly in the mining sector, it acts as a disincentive on private investment and production. Experience in Zambia, shows that anytime Government levied high tax rates on mining houses, they have downscaled production and labor, arguing that the high tax rates increases the costs of production. We have witnessed situations where as a result of the mines downscaling Copper production and laying off workers, economic activities have reduced in the mining Towns on the Copper-belt province. When hundreds of miners are laid off, this negatively affects the business activities, because income has been withdrawn from the potential customers. The demand for goods and services reduce, as a result of the reduction in the number of people who have disposable income. Therefore high tax rates may destabilize the economy. But I have proposed another way of state intervention in the industry-through increasing the shareholding of the Government in each mining house or taking over the running of certain mines where the current owners are not paying a fair share of taxes to the

Government. This can enhance revenue collection from the sector.

A commodity led industrialization program should be envisioned by the Government. A commodity led industrialization program is not a new phenomenon, oil export countries, like United Arab Emirates, Russia, Sweden and Iran have diversified their economy away from depending on oil by using oil revenues to set up competitive manufacturing and tourism industries.

Considering the fact, that as a country, we are already burdened with high debts levels, a situation that does not allow us to continue borrowing to finance developmental projects, I therefore advocate for a commodity led industrialization strategy where copper revenues can be utilized .

Of course, a commodity led diversification is only good when the metal prices are high, we can still take advantage of the boom periods (when the price of metals is high). The Copper revenues from the boom period could be used to support other sectors of the economy. Therefore the diversification framework should not be dependent entirely on revenues from the mining industry.

If the Government of Zambia can play an active role in the mining industry, we can retain a sizeable amount of revenues from the mining industry in the domestic economy, like it was in the Kaunda era.

For example, between 1964 and 1995, all metal export proceeds were channeled through the bank of Zambia. After privatization of the Metal industry, export proceeds were externalized and mining firms were free to keep their export revenues in their parent bank accounts abroad.

Having copper revenues circulate in the economy is cardinal because money supply is likely to increase which will lead to lowering of interest rates. Low interest rates will likely boost production and investment among small and medium enterprises (SMEs). The numerous small and medium sized enterprises can be more productive if they are financially supported. The dominant constraint to the expansion of these small and medium sized enterprises is the financial constraint. Small businesses in most cases do not have collateral to enable them get a loan from a lending institution. Above all, the interest rates are still high.

With Finances realized from the metal industry, the Government of Zambia can come up with a deliberate program to financially support the start-ups and small businesses so that they can also be active players in the economy to add value to our agricultural and mineral products, alongside the foreign investors. The revenues from the mining sector can be used to financially support the local small businesses.

There is no small businesses, that can grow in a vacuum-for the Zambian entrepreneurs and peasant farmers to develop, they still need financial and technical support from the Government. But the dominant constraint that limits any given Government to help its people is how rich or poor it is. The Zambia Government needs to invest in making Agriculture-and-farmers more productive. There are numerous small scale farmers who are not using their land in the most efficient way. An overhaul of the Agriculture sector in Zambia is a matter of urgency-especially given that, as the effects of climate change intensify, growing sufficient amounts of food will become more challenging in Zambia and Africa at large.

The climate has become more unpredictable, increasing the irregularity of rainfall, uncertain harvests, and as a result the risks of food insecurity. Anticipated changes in climate will only make subsistence living for the 60% of Zambians who still farm and graze animals as their primary livelihood difficult.

We should also consider that in today's world a diversification program that is silent on skills development, especially for the youths is likely to fail. Youths bulges have become a global phenomenon especially in less developed countries like Zambia. Youths in Zambia represent almost two thirds of the country's working-age population and almost one quarter of them are unemployed according to the World Bank estimates. Unless things improve, the future looks bleak.

Any failure to provide appropriate opportunities for this large segment of the population could have enormous economic, political, cultural and social consequences. If this large cohort of young people cannot find employment and earn a satisfactory income, the youth bulge will become a huge mass of frustrated youths likely to become a potential source of social and political instability. Engaging the youth population is therefore no longer a choice but an implementation in the development process.

We have so many churches in this country, however the church in this country and Christians worldwide must realize that it is not only about preaching the gospel to the youths to build them morally. The preaching of the gospel must be backed up by meaningful social actions like providing social-economic opportunities for the youths. Jesus did not limit his ministry to preaching. The Gospel shows in numerous incidents that he deeply cared for the temporal welfare of the people. He feed the hungry people that followed him into the wilderness(Mark 6:30-42) and objected to the injustices done to helpless widows.

Without such empowerment initiatives to the youths, vices will remain rampant in our society.

As Reverend Louis J. Luzbetak, S.V.D puts it in his book- The Church and cultures. He says,"The beautiful flowers of religion and morality cannot thrive where the weeds of starvation, unemployment, ignorance and injustice flourish". Therefore, this a call to action to the body of Christ in Zambia.

A strong Kwacha is favorable for the country

According to Professor Weeks of the University of London together with Dr. Mungule, Principal policy analyst of the National economic Advisory council- Lusaka,(neac) through their working paper- Tracking the Kwacha: Determinants of the Zambian Kwacha, of 2013. Their findings were that the Kwacha and copper prices have a weak negative correlation between them. This implies that the copper prices do not directly affect the Kwacha. They indirectly affect the Kwacha in the sense that, high copper prices attracts investors in the mining sector who bring foreign exchange inflows into the money market. The duo, therefore, advised the government to implement policies to encourage copper export revenues to come back to the domestic economy and benefit the domestic economy. In this way the price of copper will have a strong effect on the Kwacha.

For instance between 2002 and 2005 Zambia's total exports more than doubled from just a billion US Dollars to nearly US$ 2.1 billion; However the increase was mainly because of a rise in the price of copper, which amounted to 50% of total exports in 2005. During the same period the national currency (Kwacha) appreciated against other currencies like the US Dollar. The Government at the time which was headed by the late President,

Mr.Levy.P Mwanawasa of the Movement for Multiparty Democracy party (MMD) with his Finance minister, Mr.N'gandu Magand were praised by Zambians. The Kwacha appreciation resulted from inflows from foreign investors when the price of copper went up and because the country's risk rating drastically improved following the period when the Zambian debts were written off by multilateral institutions and bilateral creditors. There wasn't any fiscal/Monetary policies or legislation from the government that resulted in the kwacha appreciating. To this day, The Zambian Kwacha remains volatile due to so many factors, mostly external. The sad part is that Zambia, does not have an effective exchange rate stabilization policy apart from the central bank of Zambia buying the kwacha, in times when it depreciates against other major convertibles.

One way the Kwacha would have gained was the period when the Zambian Government enacted SI 33 and 55 to monitor international transactions. Since these statutory instruments required that exporters have a foreign currency account held with a local commercial bank, where their cash receipts were going to be held, while investors were required to deposit the cash of their pledged investment component in a similar account. In this way, there would have been increased inflows of foreign exchange in the economy- all the natural resources being sold were going to be receipted by the central bank and all those who wanted them could have deposited the accepted currencies at the central bank . The increased supply of the foreign currencies was going to help the kwacha gain against other major convertibles.

A strong kwacha is good for the country than a weaker kwacha, because in Zambia, a large percentage of the food supply is imported. So once the Kwacha depreciates against other convertibles, Imports become more expensive. Meaning that, as the Kwacha depreciates the prices of food and other commodities being sold on the Zambian market will rise proportionally to the increase in the costs of imports. This scenario directly affects the ability of rural poor to afford essential purchases.

Further a strong kwacha is favorable for economic diversification, simply because with a strong kwacha, equipment and inputs used in Agriculture become relatively cheaper. This can give an incentive farmers and agribusiness men and women, to purchase high tech equipment from abroad that can increase efficiency and productivity in the agricultural sector. This will likely lead to value addition in the Agricultural sector (the production of manufactured commodities) and employment generation. In this case strong kwacha will enhance value addition and job creation.

Increased food and livestock productivity can help reduce the prices of foodstuffs in the country, because local food producers will also flood the market with locally produced foodstuffs. This will increase the supply of foodstuffs in the country, which will eventually lead to a reduction in food prices. A vibrant manufacturing sector can further bring foreign exchange into the country through exports.This can further help the Zambian kwacha gain, as the kwacha gains imports of crude oil will become relatively cheaper leading to a scenario where the pump prices of fuel and petrol reduce. This reduces the cost of doing business in the country, making those industries that use fuel as a major input in their production process competitive.

MONGOLIA DOES NOT surpass Zambia in terms of copper production, but its share of fiscal revenues from the mining sector has been increasing during the boom (2003-2008) compared to Zambia. Although in 2008 when copper prices slumped, it was hit hard, it had to borrow for budgetary support. In the same period Mongolia has learnt from Chile on best practices employed in natural resources rich economies. The "boost and burst" tendency of copper prices provides a strong incentive to create a"Copper fund" similar to the petroleum fund effectively used in Norway and under considerations in other countries . Zambia could have made such a fund from revenues derived from the copper industry during the boom of (2003-2008), had we known better on how to manage our natural resources for the good of the Zambian people.

All the same, Zambia can still consider such a fund especially when we seal the loopholes used by the multinationals to avoid tax. Chile has this fund. This fund in Zambia could be used to accumulate foreign reserves and could also be used to counter-cyclical mechanism to stabilize the public sector fiscal balance and to fund public investments in a time when the price of copper has slumped on the international market. When Zambia is compared to Chile in generating revenues from copper mines, the country does not come close whatsoever to the trend picture that Chile has.

THE TABLE BELOW shows a marked difference between the two countries.

Year	Chile Copper share of Fiscal Revenue	Chile Copper Revenue/ GDP	Zambia Copper Share of Fiscal Revenue (%)	Zambia Copper1 Revenue/GDP (%)
1994	8.3%	1.6%	1.1%	0.5%
1995	12.2%	2.5%	3.0%	0.6%
1996	7.9%	1.4%	2.8%	0.5%
1997	8.5%	1.4%	3.0%	0.4%
1998	2.9%	0.5%	1.5%	0.3%
1999	3.1%	0.4%	11.8%	2.1%
2000	5.8%	0.9%	12.9%	2.8%
2001	3.4%	0.5%	11.4%	0.1%
2002	3.5%	0.5%	0.1%	0.0%
2003	6.4%	10.%	0.3%	0.0%
2004	18.6%	3.1%	0.1%	0.0%
2005	20.7%	3.8%	0.7%	0.1%
2006	31.1%	5.7%	0.7%	0.1%
2007	25.7%	4.8%	1.0%	0.2%
2008	24.6%	4.0%	3.4%	0.6%

SOURCE: DIPRES, CSO - Monthly Bulletin of Statistics, Ministry of Finance and National Planning

FROM THE TABLE we can see that there has been an increase in the fiscal income (taxation) from copper mines in the recent boom years (2003-2008) in Chile. Copper share of fiscal revenues have been in the range of 6.4% to 24.6%. On the other hand because of generous tax concessions and Transfer pricing, mining companies did not remit any reasonable mineral taxes to the Zambia state coffers. Therefore, despite the high share of copper total exports, the country still has very low revenue take from copper relative to total public revenues. This trend need to be reversed.

5

Zambia can become a Successful Welfare State if we can Experience Good Governance

If we are to go by the findings that, Zambia is losing US$3 billion annually, this is enough proof that the country can realize substantial amounts of money if it seals the loopholes .In-fact enough money to trigger a Zambian industrial revolution.

Combating transfer pricing schemes used by mining companies and other tax avoidance schemes used by other companies like Zambia Sugar require enough government capacity which is currently lacking. The country will continue losing tax revenues in this manner for as long as these schemes remain unchecked. Having seen that transfer pricing is a complex thing to deal with, especially with the fact that our tax authority (ZRA) lacks the much needed technological knowhow and skills to adjust to the changing business practices in the global world. They are not sophisticated enough to meet the challenges of modern businesses. They lack capacity possessed by the army of lawyers and accountants assembled by multinational corporations. It is for this reason why the Zambia Revenue Authorities (ZRA) contracted the Norwegian Tax Auditors in 2009 to investigate tax avoidance in Zambia. This is a clear sign that we lack the capacity to do it ourselves.

Even civil society, industry experts and government officials have voiced out the same concern that Zambia Revenue (ZRA) technical understanding of mining is still not adequate given the sectors economic significance and the potential for tax avoidance.

According to one NGO, it is on record saying-" A guy with a chartered account qualifications understand the general rules of taxation but mining is like Aeronautics, you need an industry background to interpret figures correctly". Although western countries like Norway have come on board to help Zambian tax personnel get the necessary skills to meet the challenges of transfer pricing, it might take many years for us to be at par in knowledge and skills with the developed countries .Copper mining can be a profitable business especially when the copper prices are high.

We have looked at estimates which says that Zambia could be losing US$3billion in tax avoidance, in a year because some multinational corporations avoid paying corporate tax. In this case we are talking of taxes. Suppose the Zambian government was the one running some mines and making the huge profits made by the mines, Zambia would in very few years achieve the status of middle income country, provided we prudently use the financial resources for the economic and social development of the country.

What I mean is that Zambia needs a new model of state intervention in the economy. Why can't the government consider running a mine or two in order to maximize on generating revenues from the mining industry which can be used to accelerate the economic and social development agenda of the country?-unlike the current situation where the benefits from the mining industry do not accrue to the Zambian populace but to foreign investors.

We are at a time in history where decisions we take today will influence the lives of generations to come. And just like in everything else in life, we have two choices. We can choose to sit back and watch or take action. We can sit and allow the greedy minds of the owners of Glencore and Vedanta complete their agenda of economically enslaving Zambians.

If Zambia can run a mine or two for the sole purpose of extracting as much revenues as possible to stimulate production in other sectors of the economy, then Zambia can become a successful Welfare state.

The welfare state is a concept of Government in which the state plays a key role in the protection and promotion of the economic and social wellbeing of its citizens.

Modern welfare states include Scandinavian countries like Germany, France, Belgian and the Netherlands. The Nordic countries such as Iceland, Sweden and Norway are also welfare states. The welfare state involves a transfer of funds from the state to Government services provided and to individual citizens for economic and social reasons. Zambia can pursue policies of the welfare state to redistribute income from the metal industry to other sectors of the economies or in order to improve the delivery of social services like Health and Education to the Zambian people and stimulate production in key sectors like Agriculture and manufacturing.

Although, the World Bank and other lending institution have been calling for the shrinkage of the state's role in the economy arguing that state intervention hurts economic growth. If state intervention hurts economic growth, how can it be that South Korea's economy grew rapidly despite the state's intervention in that economy? So when I say government should run a mine, am I saying we should go back to the classical socialist policies that President Kaunda pursued? No, that would hurt the economy.

Am calling for a mixed Economy where the Government

is playing an active role in the economy while private enterprises remain vibrant. It is still a market based economy with numerous players that also includes public enterprises.

I have keenly followed the debate on socialism in this country especially since the 2016 political campaigns and elections. The Rainbow party Secretary General, Mr. Winter Kabimba and the Socialist Party Presidential candadate, DR. Fred M'membe have championed the socialist agenda, claiming it has the potential to transform this country.

However I feel the promulgators of Socialism in this country have not explained what type of socialism they are talking about, no wonder they have been misunderstood by the majority of Zambians.

While it is true that the neo-liberal policies have failed to make a dent on the high levels of poverty in Zambia, therefore we need to look at other economic models of growth,that can bring inclusive development, still, if the Zambian Socialists are talking about the pure Lenin or Marxist socialism, then it is not appropriate in this time and age.

I think the 21st century socialism is a hybrid, where Government is involved in a few sectors of the economy and leave othersectors to the private sector. It is not about the government running entirely all sectors of the economy. What we need is a mix of capitalist and socialist policies.

Chile has a state owned enterprise called CODELCO which owns 17% of global copper reserves and which competes with other private copper mining companies in the country. This company is running efficiently, contrary to some theories that state owned companies are less efficient. We can learn from the Chilean experience on managing state copper company. Zambia can learn a lot from Chile on how to sustainably manage natural resources so that the benefits of having copper deposits can accrue to the Zambian people.

Therefore the argument that the state's involvement in the economy discourages foreign investment in the sector does not hold up in the light of historical evidence. For example When Chile began to run its state owned copper mining company, foreign investment continued to flow in the mining sector because the state established a code for coexistence.

A second argument against the presence of the state in in productive activities is that these can only be carried out more effectively by the private sector. The classic response to this question is that the presence of a state owned copper mining company implies that the state, and hence all of its citizens, receive income from the exploitation of deposits. For example Chile's CODELCO is very efficient because it belongs to the first quartile of lower costs in the world. This efficiency has been assured by tight monitoring and audit mechanisms to ensure that CODELCO conforms to international best industrial practices to the extent where the state owned company contributes more to state coffers than all private companies combined.

Another classic example of state owned enterprises running efficiently and not need being the locus of corruption is the case of Norway. It has half of Europe's oil and gas reserves and in 2004 became the third largest exporter of oil in the world.

In the nineteenth and early twentieth centuries, Norway was so poor that 15 percent of its population emigrated, in search of more opportunities and better lives. However, with the discovery of oil and gas reserves things improved in the country.

The oil industry has been controlled by the Norwegian government through their state owned enterprise. Since 1990, Norway has been saving some of the money it receives from its oil exports in a sovereign wealth fund. As of June 2007, the fund was worth US$300 billion or US$62,000 for every Norwegian citizen. In the same year of 2007, it had the third-highest GDP per capita in the world, average life expectancy at birth was eighty years, and it ranked second in the United Nations human development index.

Norway has used the revenues from the oil industry to diversify its economy, preparing for a time when its oil runs out and so avoiding the "trap" that many African nations might find themselves into if they continue to heavily depend on a single natural resource.

We are human beings just like the people of Chile and Norway who have managed to efficiently run their state enterprises. We have people who have acquired skills on how to manage mines, 90% of the workers in the mines are Zambians, it is only some top positions which are held by expatriates. We can mobilize ourselves once more because we are capable of creating our own realities. Zambia will outlive us all. It is our country and the resources we have are God given and they are finite. Our fight then must be to ensure that we bequeath our nation to the coming generation as a going concern, not a bankrupt entity.

While some Zambians have expressed negative feelings on the state managing a copper mine because of the way the Kaunda administration through the state enterprise ZCCM was mismanaged to the extent where it began making losses. Yes we should learn from the mistakes made in the Kaunda era. Mismanagement, political patronage and falling copper prices were major causes of ZCCM collapse. After nationalization of the mines in 1970, the government increased its capital spending in mining because of the high metal prices. However after 1976, which saw the decrease in the price of copper, investment in the mines and output reduced rapidly. This reduction was due to falling copper prices and mostly because of engaging in political patronage where the company involved itself in non-profitable ventures.

Take for example the chairman of ZCCM was a party cadre, a member of the ruling party supreme policy making body. Therefore most decisions were influenced by political motives, completely overshadowing any technical advice provided by the experts. This is the same scenario we have witnessed in the country when heads of public enterprises are political appointees; some of their decisions are influenced by political motives. The Copper mines state owned company started to increase its costs despite low metal prices resulting in huge losses.

The company began to invest in socially and economically non-viable activities-like using its resources to maintain the presidential state run luxury holiday resorts.

ZCCM-IH was a major provider of social services(schools, hospitals, housing, etc) in the mining areas, this further added to its expenses. At the same time, the mines never received adequate recapitalization nor undergo Modernization.

The mining sector became an important job generator for

political purposes, for the ruling political party to remain popular. In the 1980s more than 16% of the Zambian people worked in the mining sector. Further the engagement of ZCCM in non-core activities expanded the labor force raising labor related costs against a backdrop of low copper prices and revenues. As a result of falling metal prices and rising production costs the company's revenue shrank and the company made huge losses.

The increase in production costs made it impossible to retain surplus for further investment to improve the equipment so that production increases. Therefore in the 1980s and 1990s the level of copper production in Zambia decreased to an annual rate of -3.4% to -5.0% per year. It was after 2000 that the new Zambia copper mine owners reversed the downward trend. After 1990s the state owned company continued to make losses. The diagram below shows ZCCM financial statement between 1990 -1998.

Table III. 1: ZCCM – Consolidated Financial Position (US$ million)

Year	Sales	Cost of sales	Net Profit/(Loss)
1990	915.58	711.76	82.06
1991	881.11	663.66	80.53
1992	560.12	532.95	23.83
1993	666.95	554.67	91.72
1994	583.51	851.62	(108.66)
1995	692.20	1,165.61	3.98
1996	1,322.21	1,223.83	(24.91)
1997	1,149.46	1,188.15	(151.80)
1998	699.12	825.61	(251.39)

Source: ZCCM Financial Statements (Various

Source: ZCCM Financial Statements (Various

These losses made in the late 1990s provided a good reason to privatize the state owned mining company.

6

Leadership is Key

Nevertheless, success will not be automatic just because there is some involvement by the government in running a copper mine or mines. Issues related to governance, Transparency and accountability over the revenues generated will remain central. If Zambia can get this balance right, then the country's mineral wealth can finally begin to contribute to its long term economic and social development agenda.

Bringing people in top leadership position who will fight vices like corruption will set a good foundation for efficient service delivery, economic growth, capacity building for the youths, etc. We need to realize that we cannot build anything solid without a good foundation. A good foundation is imperative for any nation to achieve its set goals.

Experience in Africa shows that moneys from natural resources can flow into the state coffers without much effect to the rest of the population . In most cases the ruling elite is not willing to share the revenues from the natural resources with the broader population.

Consider Equatorial Guinea, an oil rich nation and a non-democratic country with a one party state governance system. Most businesses in that country are owned by Government officials and members of their families. Oil resource has made those who run the country, to be extremely wealth, but most of the people are still poor subsistence farmers.

Nigeria is another country which offers a classic example of how poor leadership can facilitate the exploitation of a commodity,at the expense of the vast majority of a country's people's.

Because of the competition for oil revenues, Nigeria has experienced political violence,social unrest, long periods of military rule, massive corruption and extreme poverty. Significant portions of oil revenues have been looted by the leaders themselves,making a mockery of the fact that oil resources are meant to benefit all Nigerians not just a few individuals.

A French Newspaper estimated that from 1989 to 1998, the back to back Nigeria leaders Ibrahim Babangida and

Sani Abacha accumulated $8billion between them. This is not an insignificant amount. Recovering the "Abacha loot"has been a major priority for Nigeria.I n 2008, $500 million was returned to Nigeria from Sani Abacha's Swiss Accounts.

On 05 December,2017(source BBC) The Swiss Government announced that it was going to return $320m of the money allegedly stolen by Nigeria's late ruler Sani Abacha. The late ruler is suspected to have embezzled about $2.2bn from Nigeria's central bank.

This is why some academicians are skeptical towards development driven by natural resources in Africa. They argue that dreaming of developing an African country through natural resources is a deadly fantasy. Experience shows it might help a few people in power, or, in other cases the urban upper middle class to get rich, but it will not improve the living conditions of the huge majority of the people.

This is also the reason why so many rich resource countries in Africa have failed to provide basic needs to the majority of their people. It is for this reason why despite generating massive revenues from natural resources, many resource rich nations still have pathetic healthcare systems with a high infant mortality rate.

The relationship between GDP and infant Mortality rate is

extremely important, though negated by western academicians. According to the most UN human rights texts, decreasing infant mortality is part of the human rights obligations of each government.

The diagram below shows the relationship between GDP and Infant Mortality rate in resource rich countries.

The black line represents the linear regression between the two variables. In other words, this is the line for which the sum of the squares of the vertical distances between the line and the various points is minimal. It allows us to calculate the average Infant Mortality Rate which we would expect for a certain level of GDP Level. If a country is significantly below the line, then, it has provided a better than-than-average survival chances for the babies born there. If a country is significantly above the line, we can consider that its achievements in the field of health care are questionable.

The Chart Below shows countries which massively export oil or mining products

Courtesy of rainbowbuilders.org

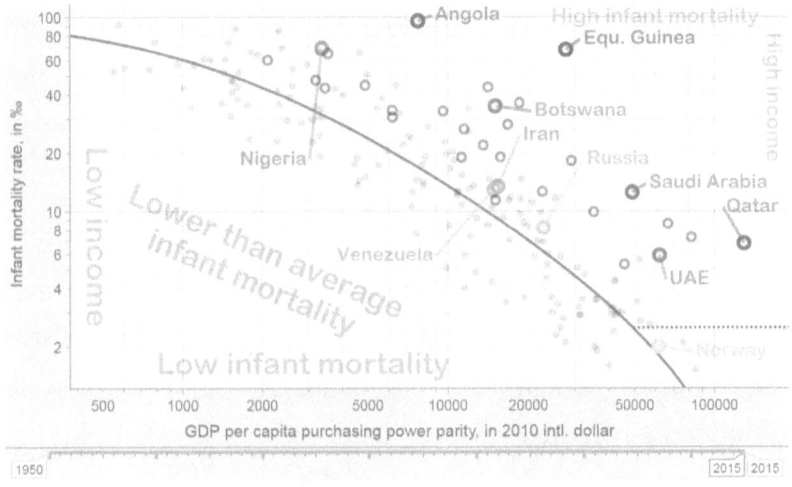

From the above chart it is only Norway that has utilized revenues from its natural resources to improve their health care system, hence the low infant Mortality rate. Except for Norway, none of the oil and mining exporting countries have got a better-than average health care system. This can be linked to poor governance system in these countries.

Therefore if Zambia should consider running a state mine so that financial fruits from the metal industry are equitably distributed, Zambia needs to experience good governance, on top of being called a Christian Nation.

For example, Zambians are always proud of their country because it is a Christian nation and a peaceful nation on the African continent because we have never had any civil war or civil unrest. But what many Zambians do not understand is that peace is not just the absence of war in any nation.

The absence of war or civil unrest is not the only phenomenon that characterizes peace, but the presence of justice too, and in this case economic justice. Peace also entails justice and upholding of human rights. Likewise democracy requires various freedoms and leveled playing fields and thousands of bills of rights and civil liberties.

However Peace alone has not brought economic prosperity to our land, Zambia. There are certain countries like Angola which underwent political instability for decades but after the war ended her economy has been performing better than that of Zambia, a nation that has been at peace and has known no war.

Angola's economy has experienced rapid growth. In 2007, increased demand and a high price for Angola's daily production of 1.5 million barrels of oil meant that the country's GDP expanded by 21% that year alone. The capital of Angola, Luanda has been undergoing a construction boom and hotel occupancy rates are nearing 100%. From Angola's story we can learn that to attract investment we need a good business environment apart from political stability in that country. Economic justice is a human right.

However If we are going to have a state run mine like Chile we must ensure that the people we elect to positions of leadership and power are people of integrity who would be custodians of our national wealth with accountability and Transparency.

We need to remember that one factor that made the copper mining state owned company ZCCM to collapse was political patronage, fuelled by mismanagement of the affairs of the company at the highest level of management. Unless we embrace the challenge of leadership in our country, theft of public resources and corruption will remain rife in this country.

If we have corrupt leaders at the top and people in the country realize that their political leaders are not honesty, even the most honesty people at the grassroots lose the motivation to root out the scourge of corruption. The Bemba proverb **Isabi Ukubola Libalila Kumutwe,** means, A fish rots head downwards -. This means a society works like a machine, if one of the parts of the machine cogs jams, this will affect the performance of other parts of the machine. This means that when people no longer have the trust in their political system, because they have realized that, the politicians are not honesty; economic sabotage becomes the norm among citizens of that country. If the subordinates in government institutions know that their superiors are looting, what can stop them from doing so as well? No matter how many times senior officials in government warn others against corruption, if they are not walking the talk, no one will take them serious. Year in and year out, the auditor's general report shows massive misappropriation of public funds and abuse of office among public workers but nothing has been done satisfactory to deal with corrupt elements in the system. There have been calls by various stakeholders for the government to give constitutional powers to the Auditor General's office to prosecute people who have been implicated in their report. Such calls have fallen on deaf ears and no measures have been taken to this day to deal with corrupt elements in the system that is implicated in corrupt activities. This shows that we do not take the issue of corruption serious in our country.

Mind you, not talking from a Christian perspective but from a purely economic point of view, corruption is worse than prostitution because while prostitution endangers the morals of an individual, corruption endangers the morals of the entire country. While Prostitution puts the prostitute at risk, corruption places the innocent at a huge disadvantage. Corruption equals poverty, lack of equipment and medicines in hospitals, lack of desks and textbooks for pupils in schools and many other social amenities for the citizens throughout the country. This is because the money that was supposed to provide these services to the people has been pocketed by a few people.

In order to get rid of corruption we need to emphasize that we need strong institutional structures and not only strong politicians. The only way our country can move forward in fighting corruption is by strengthening our institutions. If our institutions were strong enough, many of those who have abused authority, but have gone scot free because they have connections in Government, would not be there in the community because they are danger to society. Many Citizens have raised concern that a situation where directors of most watchdog institutions are political appointees is not alright, because, political appointee have a double agenda- to please the people and the appointing Authority. Many argue that The Ant-Corruption Commission is failing to perform their noble duties because of interference from political leaders. Therefore let we need to amend the constitution in such a way that the executive will have no part in the appointment, discipline and removal of certain watchdog's institutions. That way these institutions will become strong, in the sense that, they will be immune from politicians

Therefore if this country of ours Zambia is to prosper we need principled and visionary leadership that will put the interest of the Zambian people first. However Leadership is not simply a matter of filling the top positions in a government institution or private business. Nor is it a quality restricted to the ambitious, the elite, the personally gifted, or highly educated. In fact, leadership can be demonstrated by those who are marginalized and poor as much as by those who have had all the privileges that society has been able to bestow on them. Perhaps the most important quality that the Zambian leadership needs to embrace and which is desperately lacking in Zambia is a sense of service to their people.

One way to improve the leadership in this country is to reject clueless and worn-out politicians; Political harlots that have no other objective in their political agenda, but to glean as possible from the Zambian government coffers before they die. Why should these clueless politicians continue in politics when it has always been an accepted fact that power can be rightly exercised when in the hands of men and women of integrity? But the majority of our politicians lack integrity, they move from one political party to another, not realizing that Politics is about ideologies not just having a membership card of a certain political party.

The crucial but often overlooked fact is this: These clueless politicians compromise the development of the nation. They have no grasp of current issues in the world affairs and national macro-economics. Further, young men who would otherwise have taken their rightful places in the corridors of power are prevented from bringing their fresh and innovative ideas to the political table. The result is that the economy is deprived of novel and original ideas, and ends up recycling old notions that lost their efficacy sometime in the last century. I do not think there is such a bankruptcy of fresh-minded, credible people to join politics in this country. I believe it is our responsibility as Zambians to demand political temperance. The place to begin is by rejecting political prostitution, especially that being practiced by some politicians who have nothing but self-enrichment in their minds.

WE NEED politicians who are sound and who have familiarized themselves with the challenges facing the Zambian people. Let us remember that any faulty thing we see today will remain faulty if we cannot stand up and fix it.

IN MEDICINE, diseases need to be treated as early as possible after they are discovered, because there comes a time when a disease like cancer which has been left untreated for so long becomes difficult for any medical specialist to treat and inevitably the patient dies. In economics, it is equally possible for an economic situation of an entity to become so dire that no economist or business expert of whatever ability can find efficacious remedy to bring that entity back to life. This is the reason failing businesses that fail to implement recovery measures and strategies in time eventually face bankruptcy and liquidation.

We do not need leaders who play politics with ethnicity,

grab public lands, sell off natural resources, and loot the treasury or tolerate such actions by others. We need leaders who will foster values such as fairness, Justice and working for the common good rather than turning a blind eye to violence and exploitation, promoting self- interests.

7

Conclusion

My book has been written to engage Zambians into thinking objectively on how they should manage natural resources. The abundant natural resources should contribute significantly towards the social and economic development of this country. The Zambian Government can implement policies and legislation that can stop the evasion or dodging of taxes by Multinational companies. I have argued that, through a deliberate policy, the Government of Zambia can play an active role in the mining sector to maximize generating revenues from the mining sector.

In other words, my book is advocating for the redistribution of income from the mining sector to the broader population of the country. We need to change the current status quo were it is the mining investors who are mainly benefitting from the copper production in Zambia, and not the Zambian People. We need a win –to- win situation. Therefore we need to redistribute income from the mining sector to the broader population of the country, in order to reduce the inequality in income and wealth between the shareholders of the Mining companies and the Zambian people who own the resources.

Government should take the issue of redistributive justice very serious, to enhance economic and social development of the country. If it doesn't, Forward motion and Stasis will continue to occur at the same time in Zambia, particularly in the mining industry. What I mean is that Copper output from the sector, has been increasing each successive year, but has this increase in Copper production made a significant positive impact on the poor Zambians? The answer is no, from the book, we have seen that copper revenues as a share of the total public revenues has been below 1% until in the year 2008 when the share rose to 3%. This means, given the industry's potential to generate massive revenues, for the government, the linkage between the mining sector and other sectors is still very weak. This should not be so, considering the fact that Copper production remains the main stay of the economy. If well managed, the mining sector can generate substantial revenues that can contribute towards the improvement of the health, education, Tourism and Agricultural sectors.

Hence there is forward motion in the mining sector in the

sense that, we have registered an increase in Copper production, which has benefitted the investors in the sector, however, there is stasis, in the sense that, the benefits from the rise in Copper production and other minerals has not trickled down to the broader population of the Zambian people. This is why I propose that the Government should take an active role in the industry to redistribute income. A High taxation policy could be one fiscal policy the Government of Zambia can use to mobilize financial resources that can be used to accelerate economic and social development of this country. However, a high taxation policy can hamper the expansion of the industry. Tax in a developing country like Zambia has limits; if you have higher taxation levels, particularly in the mining sector, it acts as a disincentive on private investment and production. Experience in Zambia, shows that anytime Government levied high tax rates on mining houses, they have downscaled production and labor, arguing that the high tax rates increases the costs of production. We have witnessed situations where as a result of the mines downscaling Copper production and laying off workers, economic activities have reduced in the mining Towns on the Copper-belt province. When hundreds of miners are laid off, this negatively affects the business activities, because income has been withdrawn from the potential customers. The demand for goods and services reduce, as a result of the reduction in the number of people who have disposable income. Therefore high tax rates may destabilize the economy. But I have proposed another way of state intervention in the industry-through increasing the shareholding of the Government in each mining house or taking over the running of certain mines where the current owners are not paying a fair share of taxes to the Government. This can enhance revenue collection from the sector.

If public funds can increase as a result of implementing good policies to generate more revenues from the mining sector, These revenues can play a vital role provided the funds are prudently utilized. They can be used to improve healthcare system in the country, improve education system and other training programs which promote human capital formation. Human Capital formation is essential for economic and social development of a country. In order to economically develop, Zambia needs an overhaul of the education system. We need to develop a highly efficient school system(primary, high school and college/Universirty education) for the whole population with well trained teachers. A good school system is vital for the growth of the services sector. This is because the services industry needs highly educated and skilled people to make it successful.

Consider the most dynamic economies in Africa: Ethiopia, Tanzania and Rwanda. They are among the 15 most dynamic economies in the world, when they do not have significant natural resources like Zambia. Rwanda is building up an economy based largely on the services sector. Zambia can also go this way, but, but it requires a huge push in education first in order to have a chance of succeeding.

But it all comes down to the kind of political leaders we have opted for. Like I said in my book, some Academics argue that basing the development of an African country on natural resources is a deadly fantasy. Quite alright, revenues from natural resources can flow into the country's coffer. However, these revenues might just help the urban upper middle class, to get rich, but it will not improve the living conditions of the majority of the people because of lack of political will from the government to redistribute income to the broader population. Experience in most resource rich, African countries show that Corruption, tribalism and nepotism, gets into the way of sustainable natural resource management. Therefore, its up to the Zambian citizenly to put in power people of integrity- who can be good custodians of their natural resources.

BIBLIOGRAPHICAL REFERENCES AND NOTES

1. Fraser Alastair and Lungu John, Zambia-copper-mine; A study of the impact of privatization on the Zambian economy- http://www.sarpn.org/document/d0002403/1[accessed 19th November 2016]
2. Meller P. and Simpasa, "Role of copper in the Chilean and Zambian economy, copyright (2011)" a working paper no.43 GDN-global development network.
3. Curtis Mark, "War on want tax report for Zambia, 2015" A study of how Zambia is losing US$3billion from corporate tax dodging every year.http://www.gdn.int/admin/uploads/editor, [accessed 7th December 2016]
4. Readhead Alexander " Transfer pricing in the mining sector in Zambia, 2016" a case study of the

Natural Resource Governance institute. http://www.resourcegovernance.org [accessed 24, October 2016]

5. TsidiTsikala, Qiang Cui, Byung Jang, Tobias Rosmusses, Manuel Rosales and Robert Tchaidza, " An analysis of change in Zambia's mining fiscal regime, 2015" a paper for the International Monetary Fund-http://www.imf.org [accessed 12th December 2016]
6. WangariMaathai, " The Challenge for Africa, 2009" Random house inc, New York, U.S.A
7. Mungule K. Osward and Weeks John, " Determinants of the Zambian Kwacha, 2013" A working paper commissioned by International Growth Centre at the London School of Economics in partnership with Oxford University.http://www.theigc.org/wp-content/upload/2 [accessed 16 August 2015]
8. Other narrations captured by a documentary entitled Stealing Africa-Why Poverty?see www.youtube/watch
9. Sarah Freitas, Global Financial Integrity, what-billions-in-illicit and licit-capital flight means for the people of –Zambia-http://www.financialtransparency.org [accessed 22 February 2017]
10. Grant Thornton-Pilot Audit Report- Mopani copper mines, plc 2011. Available at http://www.

actionaid.org.uk/tax-justice/glencore-tax-dodging-in-Zambia.

11. Lusaka Times.2014.Videos of Vedanta Boss saying KCM makes $500 million profit per year, retrieved 8th August,2016 from https://www.lusakatimes.com/2014/03/13/video-vendanta-boss-saying-kcm-makes-500million-profit-per-year/.

12. MwalaKalaluka" KCM cheats on copper exports", the post newspaper, 4th July 2014.

13. Simpasa A, Hailu D, Levine S and Tibana R. J, " Capturing mineral Revenues in Zambia: Past trends and future prospects 2013" A discussion paper- http://www.undp.org/extractiveindustries. [accessed 14 December 2016]

14. GRZ. (2013) The bank of Zambia (monitoring of balance of payments) Regulations, 2013. Statutory instrument (SI) NO: 55. Government Printers.

www.ingramcontent.com/pod-product-compliance
Lightning Source LLC
Chambersburg PA
CBHW020449220526
45464CB00002B/926